● soho the

Soho Theatre presen

Shrieks of Laughter

by Moses Raine

First performed at Soho Theatre on 11 May 2005

Shrieks of Laughter was commissioned as part of
Soho Theatre's Writers' Attachment Programme,
supported by the Harold Hyam Wingate Foundation and
collectively supported by Soho Theatre's Dear Friends.

Soho Theatre is supported by

  Bloomberg

Performances in the Lorenz Auditorium

Registered Charity No: 267234

Shrieks of Laughter

by Moses Raine

Thomas	**Oliver Coleman**
Raymond	**Sam Cox**
Henry	**Tom Payne**
Peter	**Clarence Smith**
India	**Imogen Stubbs**
Solent Coastguard / Target One	**Nigel Betts**
Dan / Captain / Jackie / Voice One	**Christopher Hunter**
Josie / Kayliegh	**Matti Houghton**
Shelley	**Sally Orrock**
Director	**Maria Aberg**
Designer	**Jon Bausor**
Lighting Designer	**Nigel Edwards**
Sound Designer	**Matt McKenzie**
Assistant Director	**Sophie Austin**
Casting Director	**Sam Chandley**
Costume Supervisor	**Fizz Jones**
Production Manager	**Nick Ferguson**
Stage Manager	**Sarah Buik**
Deputy Stage Manager	**Marie Costa**
Chief Technician	**Nick Blount**
Chief Electrician	**Christoph Wagner**
Lighting Technician	**Mark Watts**
Scenery built and painted by	**Robert Knight Ltd.**
Press Representation	**Nancy Poole** (020 7478 0142)
Photography	**Getty Images**

Soho Theatre, 21 Dean Street, London W1D 3NE
Admin: 020 7287 5060   Fax: 020 7287 5061
Box Office: 0870 429 6883
www.sohotheatre.com

Biographies

Writer

Moses Raine *Writer*

Moses wrote *Shrieks of Laughter* at the age of 21. The play was commissioned as part of Soho Theatre's Writers' Attachment Programme 2005. Moses was shortlisted for the Verity Bargate Award 2004 for *The Survival Handbook*, which was given a Launch Pad workshop in March 2005.

Cast

Oliver Coleman *Thomas*

Oliver's theatre credits include *A Midsummer Night's Dream, Kiss Me Kate, Stags and Hens, North Greenwich, Serjeant Musgrave's Dance, The Merchant of Venice, The People's Temple, The Seagull* and *The Way of the World* (LAMDA). Television credits include *The Line of Beauty* (BBC). Film credits include *Wimbledon* (Working Title).

Sam Cox *Raymond*

Sam's theatre credits include *Arabian Nights* (ATC/Soho Theatre); *Tintin* (Barbican); *The UN Inspector* (National Theatre); *Festen* (Almeida/West End); *Serjeant Musgrave's Dance* (Oxford Stage Company); *Great Expectations* (Bristol Old Vic); *Henry V, Romeo and Juliet, Richard II, Troilus and Cressida* (RSC); *The Power of Darkness, The Revenger's Tragedy* (Orange Tree); *Sweet Dreams* (Sphinx Theatre Company); *A Doll's House* (Birmingham Rep); *Uncle Silas* (Lyric Hammersmith/Tour); *Dearly Beloved* (Hampstead/Tour); *A Bright Room Called Day* (Bush); *Insignificance, The Ruling Class* (Liverpool Playhouse); *Macbeth* and *The Jail Diary of Albie Sachs* (Young Vic). Television credits include *Doctor Who, The Last Will and Testament of Billy Two Sheds, Inspector Lynley, Holby City, Crime Traveller, Back Up, Prime Suspect* and *The Chief.*

Tom Payne *Henry*

Tom graduated form the Central School of Speech and Drama in summer 2005. His theatre credits include *Journey's End* (Ambassadors Theatre); *Class Enemy, Richard III, The Rivals, The Man who had all the Luck, A Midsummer Night's Dream* and *The Three Sisters* (Central). Television credits include *Casualty* (BBC) and *Ancient Discoveries: Ancient Ships* (Granada).

Clarence Smith *Peter*

Clarence's theatre credits include *Design for Living, Les Blancs* (Royal Exchange); *Macbeth* (Arcola); *The Storm* (Almeida); *As You Like It* (The Tokyo Globe); *The Honest Whore, The Merchant of Venice* (The Globe); *King Lear, Chasing the Moment* (Southwark Playhouse); *Love at a Loss* (Wild Iris Theatre

Co.); *Romeo and Juliet, Fuente Ovejuna, Yerma, Blood Brothers, Hiawatha* (Bristol Old Vic); *The Jamaican Airman foresees his Death, Our Country's Good, Charity Event* (Royal Court); *King Lear, Don Juan* (RSC) and *Smith* (Salzburg National Theatre). Television includes *Doctors, Holby City, The Eustace Bros., Waking the Dead, EastEnders, A Midsummer Night's Dream* and *Loved Up* (BBC); *Undercover Cops* (Blast Films/Channel 4); *Daylight Robbery* (Hewland International/ITV); *Melissa* (Diplomat Films); *Full Stretch* (Witzend/Select TV) and *The Last Detective* (LWT Drama). Film credits include *Mexican Standoff, What My Mother Told Me* (Film Four); *Star Wars* (George Lucas); *Half Moon Street* (EMI) and *Ford on Waters* (BFI).

Imogen Stubbs *India*

Imogen's theatre credits include *Hamlet* (Old Vic*); Mum's the Word, Uncle Vanya* (Albery); *Three Sisters* (Theatre Royal Bath/Nuffield); *The Relapse, Betrayal* (National Theatre); *Closer* (Lyric); *Blast from the Past* (West Yorkshire Playhouse); *A Streetcar Named Desire, Heartbreak House* (Haymarket); *St Joan* (Theatre Clwyd/The Strand); *Othello, Two Noble Kinsmen, The Rover, Richard II* (RSC); *Cabaret, The Boyfriend* (New Wolsey Theatre) and *Poison, The Oxford Review* (Edinburgh). Television credits include *Miss Marple* (ITV); *Blind Ambition* (YTV); *Big Kids, Mothertime, After the Dance, Othello, Relatively Speaking, The Rainbow, The*

Browning Version (BBC); *Anna Lee* (LWT) and *Sandra: C'est la Vie* (Canal+). Film credits include *Twelfth Night* (Trevor Nunn); *Sense and Sensibility* (Ang Lee); *Jack and Sarah* (Granada/ Polygram); *Dead Cool* (David Cohen); *True Colors* (Herbert Ross); *Fellow Traveller* (Phillip Saville) and *A Summer Story* (Piers Hagard).

Company

Maria Aberg *Director*

Maria's directing credits include *Stallerhof* (Southwark Playhouse); *Love and Money* (Young Vic Directors Project); *Audrey* (RADA); *My Best Friend* (Central Station); *A Handful of Dust* (Institute of Choreography and Dance) and *The Maids* (Judi Dench Theatre). Assistant directing credits include *The Crucible* (RSC); *Aristocrats* (RNT); *Lucky Dog, Sweetest Swing in Baseball, The Sugar Syndrome* (Royal Court); *Shakespeare Love Songs* (Globe Theatre, Neuss/ Tour) and *Romeo and Juliet* (Malmo Dramatic Theatre). Maria was senior reader at the Royal Court for two years and completed the National Theatre's Studio Directors Course in 2005.

Sophie Austin
Assistant Director

Sophie's directing credits include *Romeo and Juliet, Three for Tea, Twelfth Night,* all for the site specific theatre collective Teatro Vivo and *Oedipus the King* (Tristan Bates Theatre). Her assistant directing credits include *Good Poppy, Bad Poppy* (Young Vic); *The Water Engine* (Theatre 503/Young Vic); *Chaos* (Kali Theatre); *Dead Hands* (The Wrestling School) and *The Life of Galileo* (Word of Mouth).

Jon Bausor Designer

Jon's recent design credits for theatre include *The Soldier's Tale* (Old Vic); *The Great Highway* (Gate Theatre); *Cymbeline* (Regent's Park Open Air Theatre); *The Hoxton Story* (Red Room); *Frankenstein* (Derby Playhouse); *Bread and Butter* (Oxford Stage Company/ Tricycle); *Carver* (Arcola Theatre); *The Last Waltz season* (OSC/ Dumbfounded); *Melody, In the Bag* (Traverse); *The New Tenant, Interior, The Expectation and the Rule, Winners, The Soul of Chien-nu* (Young Vic); *Sanctuary, The Tempest* (National Theatre); *The Taming of the Shrew* (Thelma Holt/Theatre Royal, Plymouth/ No.1 Tour) and *Switchback, Possible Worlds* (Tron Theatre, Glasgow). Design credits for dance includes *Snow White in Black* (Phoenix Dance Theatre/ Sadler's Wells/Tour); *Ghosts, Before the Tempest, Sophie, Stateless, Asyla* (Linbury Theatre, Royal Opera House); *Mixtures* (Westminster Abbey/English National Ballet) and *Non Exeunt* (George Piper Dances/Sadler's Wells). Opera design credits include *The Knot Garden* (Klang-bogen Festival, Vienna); *The Queen of Spades* (Edinburgh Festival Theatre), *Cosi Fan Tutte* (Handmade Opera) and *King Arthur* (New Chamber Opera). Jon was a finalist in The Linbury Prize 2000.

Nigel Edwards *Lighting Designer*
Nigel's theatre credits include *Colder than Here, Flush, Dirty Butterfly* (Soho Theatre); *Trade, Robert Zucco, The Mysteries, Shadows, The Tempest, Victoria,* (RSC); *Some Confusions in the Law about Love, Bloody Mess, Club of No Regrets, Who Can Sing a Song to Unfrighten Me?, Speak Bitterness* (Forced Entertainment); *Clare de Luz* (Insomniac); *Pigg in Hell, Total Massala Slammer, Alone and Gregoire* (Remote Control); *The Postman Always Rings Twice* (Playhouse Theatre); *Girl in a Goldfish Bowl* (Sheffield Theatres); *The Maids* (Young Vic); *Cleansed, 4.48 Psychosis, Fallout, Ladybird, Stoning Mary, Alice Trilogy* (Royal Court); *Crave, Riddance, Sleeping Around, The Cosmo-naut's Last Message, Splendour* (Paines Plough); *Ballad of Yachiyo* (The Gate, London); *One Minute, Arabian Night, The Boy who Left Home* (ATC); *When Harry met Sally* (Haymarket); *Sexual Perversity in Chicago* (The Comedy); *Misanthrope,* (The Gate, Dublin); *Mr Heracles, Inconceivable* (West Yorkshire Playhouse); *Janufa* (WNO); and *Triumph of Love* (Almeida). Nigel's credits also include the *Insen* tour by Ryuichi Sakamoto and Carsten Nicolai.

Matt McKenzie *Sound Designer*
Matt McKenzie came to the UK from New Zealand in 1978. He toured with Paines Plough before joining the staff at The Lyric Theatre Hammersmith in 1979 where he designed the sound for several productions.

Since joining Autograph in 1984, Matt has been responsible for the sound design for the opening of Soho Theatre along with its production of *Badnuff* and *Blue Eyes and High Heels*; *Vertigo* (Guildford); *Saturday, Sunday, Monday, Easy Virtue* (Chichester); *Frame 312* (Donmar); *Iron* (The Traverse and Royal Court); *Made in Bangkok, The House of Bernarda Alba, A Piece of My Mind, Journey's End, A Madhouse in Goa, Barnaby and the Old Boys, Irma Vep, Gasping, Map of the Heart, Tango Argentino, When She Danced, Misery, Murder is Easy, The Odd Couple, Pygmailion, Things we do for Love, Long Day's Journey into Night* and *Macbeth*. For Sir Peter Hall credits include *Lysistrata, The Master Builder, School for Wives, Mind Millie for Me, A Streetcar Named Desire, Three of a Kind* and *Amedeus* (West End and Broadway). Matt was Sound Supervisor for the Peter Hall Season (Old Vic and The Piccadilly) and designed the sound for *Waste, Cloud 9, The Seagull, The Provok'd Wife, King Lear, The Misanthrope, Major Barbara, Filumena* and *Kafka's Dick*. Work for the RSC includes *Family Reunion, Henry V, The Duchess of Malfi, Hamlet, The Lieutenant of Inishmore, Julius Caesar* and *A Midsummer Night's Dream*.

Soho Theatre would like to thank:

Joe Hill-Gibbons
Sally Wares
Kettle Foods Ltd
Darren Marks
Vitra for the Eames Lounge Chair

● **soho** theatre

- ● **Produces new work**
- ● **Discovers and nurtures new writers**
- ● **Targets and develops new audiences**

Soho Theatre is passionate in its commitment to new writing, producing a year-round programme of bold, original and accessible new plays – many of them from first-time playwrights.

'a foundry for new talent ... one of the country's leading producers of new writing'   *Evening Standard*

Soho Theatre offers an invaluable resource to emerging playwrights. Our training and outreach programme includes the innovative Under 11s scheme, the Young Writers' Group (18-25s) and a burgeoning series of Nuts and Bolts writing workshops designed to equip new writers with the basic tools of playwriting. We offer the nation's only unsolicited script-reading service, reporting on over 2,000 plays per year. We aim to develop and showcase the most promising new work through the national Verity Bargate Award, the Launch Pad scheme and the Writers' Attachment Programme, working to develop writers not just in theatre but also for TV and film.

'a creative hotbed ... not only the making of theatre but the cradle for new screenplay and television scripts'   *The Times*

Contemporary, comfortable, air-conditioned and accessible, Soho Theatre is busy from early morning to late at night. Alongside the production of new plays, it is also an intimate venue to see leading national and international comedians in an eclectic programme mixing emerging new talent with established names.

'London's coolest theatre by a mile'   *Midweek*

● soho theatre

21 Dean St
London W1D 3NE
Admin: 020 7287 5060
Box Office: 0870 429 6883
www.sohotheatre.com

The Terrace Bar

The Terrace Bar on the second floor serves
a range of soft and alcoholic drinks

Email information list

For regular programme updates and offers visit
www.sohotheatre.com

Hiring the theatre

Soho Theatre has a range of rooms and spaces
for hire. Please contact the theatre managers on
020 7287 5060
or go to
www.sohotheatre.com
for further details

● soho theatre

Soho Theatre Company

Staff

Acting Artistic Director:
Jonathan Lloyd
Executive Director: Mark Godfrey

Board of Directors

Nicholas Allott – chair
Sue Robertson – vice chair
Sophie Clarke-Jervoise
Norma Heyman
Roger Jospé
Michael Naughton
David Pelham
Dr Simon Singh MBE
Roger Wingate
Christopher Yu

Honorary Patrons

Bob Hoskins *president*
Peter Brook CBE
Simon Callow
Sir Richard Eyre CBE

Writer's Centre and Education

Writers' Centre Director: Nina
Steiger
Literary Assistant: Rachel Taylor
Education and Workshop Officer:
Suzanne Gorman

Administration

General Manager:
Catherine Thornborrow
Deputy General Manager:
Neil Morris
Casting & Artistic Assistant:
Nadine Hoare
Assistant to Executive Director:
Tim Whitehead
Financial Controller: Kevin Dunn
Book Keeper: Elva Tehan

Marketing, Development and Press

Marketing and Development
Director: Jo Cottrell
Development Manager: Zoe Crick
Marketing Manager: Kelly Duffy
Press and Public Relations: Nancy
Poole (020 7478 0142)
Marketing and Development
Assistant: Vicky Brown

Box Office and Front of House

Front of House Manager:
Erin Gavaghan
Box Office and Audience
Development Manager:
Steve Lock
Box Office Assistants:
Lou Beere, Colin Goodwin,
Paula Henstock, Eniola Jaiyeoba,
Ian Marshall, Leah Read, and
Natalie Worrall
Duty Managers:
Colin Goodwin, Mike Owen,
Miranda Yates and Peter
Youthed.
Front of House staff:
Beth Aynsley, Frank Carson,
Indi Davies, Joanna Hoare,
Florian Hutter, Daniel Koop,
Ian Marshall, Harry Scott, Holly
Wareing and Annabel Wood.

Production

Production Manager:
Nick Ferguson
Chief Technician: Nick Blount
Chief LX: Christoph Wagner
Lighting Technician: Mark Watts

The Soho Theatre Development Campaign

Soho Theatre receives core funding from Arts Council England, London. In order to provide as diverse a programme as possible and expand our audience development and outreach work, we rely upon additional support from trusts, foundations, individuals and businesses.

All of our major sponsors share a common commitment to developing new areas of activity and encouraging creative partnerships between business and the arts.

We are immensely grateful for the invaluable support from our sponsors and donors and wish to thank them for their continued commitment.

Soho Theatre has a Friends Scheme to support its education programme and work in developing new writers and reaching new audiences. To find out how to become a Friend of Soho Theatre, contact the development department on 020 7478 0109, email development@sohotheatre.com or visit www.sohotheatre.com.

Sponsors: American Express, Angels the Costumiers, Arts & Business, Bloomberg, Getty Images, International Asset Management, TEQUILA\ London

Major Supporters and Education Patrons: Anthony and Elizabeth Bunker • Tony and Rita Gallagher • Nigel Gee • Goldsmiths' Company • The Paul Hamlyn Foundation • Roger Jospé • Jack and Linda Keenan • John Lyon's Charity • The Pemberton Foundation • The Foundation for Sport and the Arts • The Harold Hyam Wingate Foundation

Trusts and Foundations: Anonymous • Hyde Park Place Estate Charity • The Ernest Cook Trust • The St James's Trust • The Kobler Trust • The Mackintosh Foundation • The Mercers' Company • Unity Theatre Trust

Dear Friends: Anonymous • Jill and Michael Barrington • Brin and Sian Bucknor • David Day • John Drummond • Madeleine Hamel • Michael and Mimi Naughton • Carolyn Ward.

Friends: Thank you also to the many Soho Friends we are unable to list here. For a full list of our patrons, please visit www.sohotheatre.com

Registered Charity: 267234

Moses Raine
Shrieks of Laughter

faber and faber

First published in 2006
by Faber and Faber Limited
3 Queen Square, London WC1N 3AU

Typeset by Country Setting, Kingsdown, Kent CT14 8ES
Printed in England by Bookmarque Ltd, Croydon, Surrey

A CIP record for this book
is available from the British Library

ISBN 0–571–23423–2
ISBN 978–0–571–23423–3

2 4 6 8 10 9 7 5 3 1

To my Mum and my best friend, Nicky

Acknowledgements

I would like to thank the following people:
my family, Nana and Grandpa, Mel Kenyon,
Francis Wyndham, Susannah Clapp, Patrick Hunter,
John Bails, Nancy Harris, Maria Aberg, Nina Steiger
and everyone at the Soho Theatre

Characters

India
A woman in her late forties. Eccentric dress sense,
incredibly skinny and brown

Raymond
India's husband, sixty. Short. A high-pitched laugh
only the very rich can afford

Thomas
Their eldest son. Lanky. Masculine behaviour,
just the way he sits

Henry
Their younger son. Small, slightly effeminate

Peter
Black, deep voice

There are five voices that come from radios.
Voice One is that of a newsreader.
The others are people communicating from
separate yachts over VHF radio: they are
**Lindsay Ann, Solent Coastguard,
Target One** and **Jackie**

Settings
Minimal, created mainly through sound and light

SHRIEKS OF LAUGHTER

SCENE ONE

A room. A dim lamp with a red lampshade shows Peter standing by a recliner chair. He turns to Henry, who sits in another recliner chair and looks at him hard. Peter looks at his watch.

Peter I think it's time, shall we begin, Henry?

I think you're quite relaxed enough now.

Beat.

How do you feel, young man? Would you say you're relaxed?

Henry Suppose um yeah, yes, I am.

It's very warm . . . a warm warm room, isn't it?

Peter Is it?

Henry Yeah man, it's very warm, I could almost curl up and, and go sleep.

Peter sits down.

Peter Mm.

Henry laughs. Silence.

Look me in the eye.

Look at me.

Beat.

Now . . . tell me, tell me this . . . what do you want?

Beat.

Henry Me?

Peter Do you want to look at me?

Henry Um . . .

Sorry?

Peter You've got a choice, we can do this face to face, or looking at the view?

Henry (*relieved*) Oh . . . a choice . . . I'll take the garden.

   Beat.

Peter Tell me, what can you see, I can see the trees, what can you see?

Henry I can see trees, there are the tops of trees and houses, and more, more houses, just the houses and all these trees /

Peter There're a great many trees and tops of houses, I do like the view . . . with all the trees, without their leaves . . . I think it's very beautiful.

Henry Yes.

Peter Though, one tree stands out for me, one stands out in particular.

Henry The green one, at the back.

Peter It really stands out, doesn't it? The only one with any leaves, an evergreen – uncross your arms . . . that's better, really look at it. Focus everything . . . In this light, this dark green, a most amazing dark green. If you stare at it hard enough . . . stare at it really hard and you almost want to touch it – can you touch it?

Henry Mm.

Peter A lot of pine cones, hanging on the branches.

Henry The pine cones . . . heavy.

Peter Yeah, look at how heavy they are.

Henry Weighing the branches . . .

Peter Don't talk any more. Choose a pine cone.

Nod to me, nod when you have chosen one.

After a moment, Henry nods.

Focus on it, concentrate everything on that single pine cone, listen to me as I continue to talk, follow my instructions, see that pine cone, every segment, can you see it? Can you count them? Soak in all the details . . . Really stare at it.

Breathe in very calmly, slowly breathing in through your mouth . . . slowly breathing out through your nose. Look . . . at the pine cone, let your breathing get heavier.

(*Long and calm.*) Totally relaxed, arms uncrossed, totally relaxed, breathing totally calm . . . Relax your knees. (*Two second pause.*)

Relax your calves. (*Two second pause.*)

Really relax your whole body, let go, feel your body getting limp . . . (*Two second pause.*)

Imagine that you're standing at the top of a spiral staircase. (*Three second pause.*)

Create that staircase for me, Henry. (*Three second pause.*)

Let's create a carpet for the staircase. (*Three second pause.*)

We're walking down the spiral staircase. Feel the carpet on your feet, isn't it soft?

And as you tread down, turning around and down-nn . . . carry on down, feel the weight of your eyelids, they are very heavy . . . (*Sighs.*) You are very sleepy.

Henry sniggers, but Peter interrupts him, overriding his snigger with the dull monotony of his voice.

You're laughing because you are nervous /

Henry (*dopey*) It's just you said I'm very sleepy – I'm not.

Peter No . . .

Henry breathes heavily.

Henry (*drowsy*) No . . .

Peter What a nice sensation, lids of your eyes are as heavy as pine cones. Feel the weight pulling on the branches . . . Nothing matters any more . . . Your eyelids fall like autumn leaves . . . You're very sleepy, no longer able to focus on the pine cone any more. Shut your eyes.

Two second pause. Henry shuts his eyes.

The muscles in your neck are heavy, all the muscles in your whole body . . .

(*Long.*) Everything is so relaxed.

Henry's head slumps to one side. The lights fade at a gradual speed.

Into perfect darkness, we walk, we wander . . . spiralling down the staircase into the perfect darkness, to be found by His love, held in His arms and touched by His hands . . . Washed of all sins, found and forgiven . . . Look . . . there's a woman. Whose face is it that looked up? Her face is looking up at you, her hand moving like a child swimming to the surface of a pool. That child will never get to the surface. When she talks . . . it now makes no sense at all. Just bubbles under water. But her eyes are wide open, rolling, like a child learning to focus. Wave your keys over them. Father Jerome shall swing the censer. In the perfect darkness we shall . . . to dreams that stir . . .

Pitch darkness, total blackout.

We will walk with her, into the nothingness . . . where in the wilderness . . . a small child is born, crawling into the desert where no sound can be heard, nothing grows or stirs, no birds, flowers or sea, no wind in the trees, no light from stars in the sky, no moon, no there's no moon here, we are just beyond blackened darkness . . . into the black abyss we shall slip, do not fight it, pulling you, a place that is without a time, mouth open, tumbled into the void, and everything disintegrates into the past . . . In the end we will all disappear as strangely as we appeared.

Your breath, feel it, falling tumbling heavy . . . into a century of sleep.

A century of sleep . . .

Silence, nothing but blackness.

SCENE TWO

A door opens, throwing a crack of light. Enter Figure through the door. Figure gropes for a light switch; finding it, we hear the click of the switch. A naked light bulb fuses instantly, a flash, and we are thrown back into total darkness. Figure groans. The sound of a light switch being repeatedly switched on and off, but no light comes on. Figure crosses the stage, there is a clatter as some bathroom scales are kicked. Figure yelps, moaning tetchily. Figure hobbles across the stage. Figure urinates, with a sigh. The urine comes in chattering phrases. Figure finishes, drip-dribble-drop . . . flushing of a loo, then . . . Figure starts to exit slowly, still moaning. The door is shut, the crack of light disappears. Sound of another door opening. India's voice in the distance, it seems soft. A short conversation follows, muffled but in some way apologetic, just in the tone of the voices. A bird sings, then silence.

SCENE THREE

A garden in the countryside, late evening. Silhouette of four people sitting in moonlight. During this scene Henry sits and watches, though when he speaks his family cannot hear him.

India Hen, Henry . . . Hen, come down, darling!

Raymond Leave him alone.

India I want him to come down. Hen! Henry!

Raymond Leave him, bugger off and let him sleep.

India No. Henry!

  Beat.

I'm worried about him. As much as it may sound amusing, you know um we can all laugh at stories . . . A couple of nights ago he comes into my bedroom, um. Comes in, must've been about eleven-thirty – head wobbling all over the place, must've had a couple of pints.

Can he shoot at the door! 'Hen, it's past eleven darling, is that really necessary?'

Raymond (*wry*) Surprised you needed to ask such a moronic question.

India It's of utmost importance. Wouldn't mind if he hadn't started sleepwalking /

Raymond Locked all his BBs in the gun cabinet.

India That night he didn't sleep well – um constantly worrying about it all.

I find him in the morning. As if a bomb's dropped – clothes everywhere, books over the floor. His duvet somewhere in outer space! 'Darling, how did you sleep?'

Not very well. I ask him what he dreams about, but he can't remember. He cannot for the life of him remember what on earth went on. And it scares him, I know it does.

Thomas He told me he's scared /

India God, no darling, he is, I told him to write a diary every time he does it. I said just darling note down when, what's happening in his waking life, you know, I'm sure it's connected. Um I'm sure this is a phase. But when I ask him he says it's cool, he doesn't mind.

Raymond I had a word with the sub-warden –

India And the housemaster's a nightmare, runs an incredibly tight ship, won't let boarders stay out on Saturday nights. Come on, really ridiculous, what Hen needs is the warmth of family life.

Thomas Did me a world of good.

Raymond I rang the sub-warden up, had a word /

India Wouldn't budge for all the tea in China.

Raymond Tit-head.

India It's very strange um – I get up at six to do my yoga and he's up playing computer games.

Thomas Did you ask him, he's alright?

India Well he said he was fine. I asked him if he wanted some muesli . . .

Raymond No, no. He'll pass, thank you very much.

India There's something in his eyes, something . . . It's just er not normal to be up at that hour. Leave him to it – do my yoga in the garden. There's something definitely wrong . . .

Thomas puts his hand out.

Thomas Shh . . .

Beat. Thomas takes a breath.

(*Almost smiling, soft.*) Listen . . . listen up . . . he's crying in his sleep.

India He does that a lot.

Raymond What a fantastic ear you've got . . . miraculous.

After chapel on Sunday. There's Hen, waiting in the rain . . . Delighted to see me, there he is, soaked through, but big smiles all round –

India We had a marvellous day, lots of fun. But um – and it's getting to six. Oh, I don't want to ruin it all, but I need to know when he's meant to get back. Tell him Dad could possibly give him a lift back at ten /

Raymond That would be great! Of course, he doesn't say that, mumbles something . . .

India We had supper and dropped him back afterwards as promised.

Raymond Just before he gets out of the car, we're sitting there. I put my hand on his jersey, but he's not really listening.

India Henry, whenever . . . whenever you need the sanity of home life – call us. He will, yes, that'd be good.

Raymond He walks back to house, his shoulders down . . .

Thomas Why were his shoulders down?

India Because he was sad.

Raymond Why was he sad?

Thomas We don't know.

India It was a mystery.

Raymond It is a mystery to me . . .

Thomas My mother used to make nasturtium sandwiches.

Beat.

India Now he spends Sundays walking round the empty school re-reading notice boards. Watching the wind in the cloisters blowing sheets of paper from other people's files. That's not even the half of it. Cynthia?

What's that noise? Did Cynthia call for me?

Thomas I don't think so.

India Poor old Cynthia's got arthritis, can't use the stairs any more. Can barely move from her bed. Lies like a beached whale in front of the TV.

Beat.

Thomas Is he coming with us this summer?

India He came last year.

Thomas I hope he does. Every night after Dad had gone to bed, we played cards – chatted like this /

India I'd follow Dad to bed later. Say one in the morning.

Thomas He wouldn't let on.

India 'Henry, ring, if you want to use the phone.' No, it's not necessary – um . . . So results, results. I said I'd ring up in the morning, find out what he'd got. I rang up Mr James.

Raymond A very gentle man . . . he should lose the beard.

India Shouldn't he, much nicer clean-shaven. What a lovely, down to earth . . . and so understanding. Well, Hen got straight As. After all the worrying /

Thomas Hadn't done too bad, better than me. Night before, said they'd all be Cs and Ds.

Henry I did really well, didn't I?

India But what about his parents, did he call them and let them know how he did?

Thomas Face totally changed.

India No, not necessary – it's not necessary he said . . .

Henry Because I was with you and I told you and we had champagne.

A telephone rings.

Raymond A telephone rings, Mum and Dad aren't in but his brother is, he picks the phone up.

Thomas Two second phone call! He doesn't let on about the results. No communication.

Henry I was with you! I didn't have to ring anyone!

India What does his sister do?

Henry I don't have a sister.

Thomas She's a doctor, a medical genius.

Raymond A medical genius. There you go . . . and a telephone rang.

Thomas My mother made me nasturtium sandwiches.

India He doesn't talk about his parents. He doesn't mention them to a soul. There is something very strange. (*Nodding to Thomas.*) Hand him a bottle of wine, gone within seconds. Here is a boy who wakes at five, ya . . . Here is a boy who is obviously unhappy for no good reason.

Raymond Henry, what's the big plan after school?

Thomas He wants to have a gap year.

India Been all for a gap year but then Dad made disapproving noises.

Raymond He wants to join the army, just like me.

Thomas Well that's a bad idea, the army's a fucking shit hole.

Henry I wasn't allowed to go on a gap year, Dad wanted me to join the army.

Raymond The stability of an institution.

India The army isn't a stable institution.

Thomas It's a fucking shit hole.

   Beat.

Mum, she's fine. She'd call . . .

India I can hear Cynthia calling for us. Will no one go and check on her?

   *The wind stirs in the trees, throwing a security light
   on, it lights the figures from behind.*

Everything adds up now . . . he was forced to join the army, not wanting to call us, he would wake at five – poor lamb would lie there in his bed and cry. And if he did not wake, he would walk, through sleepless dreams . . . re-reading notice boards, and the wind in the cloisters, his mother would find him in the morning, as if a bomb had dropped. Books everywhere, duvet somewhere in outer space.

Cynthia was put down, he cried for days on end.

   The security light turns off.

Raymond He treated her like his best friend.

India He gave her all the respect you'd give a human.

Thomas He wouldn't stop crying –

Raymond We buried her in the orchard, under a pear tree. For days afterwards Hen complained about it.

Thomas Claimed her body should have been embalmed.

India Jolly solemn ceremony um, we all stood there and Hen sang a hymn, and I read a poem. Ray took place of vicar and said a small prayer. Afterwards we all chucked a handful of earth over her.

Raymond The earth was cold and damp.

Thomas My fucking feet are so cold, is anyone else?

Raymond It's fucking nippy.

India Darlings, put the heater on.

Henry That's right.

Thomas God damn, my legs are numb. (*He stands up and rubs his legs.*) Freezing my tits off.

Raymond I'm going to sue for damages /

Thomas (*as he exits*) When I get my hands on fucking management, seriously this is ridiculous. Leave the sun out, you fucking bastards!

> *The silhouettes disappear into black. Dim sound of schoolboy laughter in cloisters builds, then this is replaced by the sound of seagulls, water lapping the sides of boats, nudging them against the quay. The high whistling of wind cutting and slapping ropes against the masts of yachts.*

SCENE FOUR

A voice in pitch dark.

Voice One West Pharaohs, north four or five, becoming variable three or four, showers dying out. Now the weather reports from coastal stations for 2300 GMT. Haberdashery Private, north-west circular, mainly fair, mainly good. Sister Victoria Light Vessel Automatic, north when north, occasionally gales, westerly eight, eleven miles, a thousand and fourteen. Concert Scales, rising more slowly by hand two, more than thirty-eight miles, a thousand and sixteen. Now for the weather forecast for the inshore waters of St Pollux Point, valid for the following twenty-four hours, including Spearmint to Haberdashery Private, wind north becoming variable three or four, then south-easterly four or five, nearer six, possibly seven, even eight, continuous heavy showers in west, storms . . .

SCENE FIVE

The foredeck of a Nelson (large motor boat). Early evening. Although it's late August, the sky is grey. Raymond sits drinking a glass of Pimms. Raymond drinks fairly continuously throughout this scene, pouring himself drinks as and when he wishes. India lights herself a cigarette. Henry stares at them, bewildered. Raymond laughs.

Voice One (*continues*) Laughter, moderate or good. Visibility dying out. Mood swings, north four or five, becoming variable seven or eight. (*Fading out.*) The general situation, a ridge of high pressure extends from the Pharaohs . . .

23

Raymond Stupid old bugger, ninny really pushed his luck too far this time.

India Stupid man, using his Hoover in the garden um there'd been only a few stray leaves. They butchered that lovely horse chestnut.

Raymond Precious fart.

India Angela was on the first floor putting clothes away, in um a drawer. You know, heard a noise /

Raymond The violent sound of screaming /

India Looked out of the window, well who's there but Roger hoovering the leaves up. She yells at him to stop it um /

Raymond Next minute Roger's plonked it in a puddle and he's doing the YMCA.

Raymond violently waves his arms above his head. They shriek with laughter.

India The man couldn't see. (*Puts her hand out at arm's length.*) You know, blind as a bat. Only just had laser surgery, last time we went round –

Raymond Rather fun evening, if my memory serves me correctly.

India They told Ray that he should follow suit, have it done.

Raymond Not the bloody best advert, blind bugger never saw the puddle.

They shriek with laughter.

Henry Remember when I touched the electric fences. That caned big time, thought someone'd kicked me up the arse.

(*A recollection.*) I think, didn't I . . . shit my pants.

Beat.

India (*relaxed*) Oh, that's better. That's much better, lovely bit of sun . . . mm . . .

Raymond Roger's family is actually Scottish. Estate's . . . a good seventy-something hectares of fantastic shooting, somewhere north of the border /

India (*half-sung*)
Somewhere over the rainbow, way up high,
There's a land that I heard of, once in a lullaby.
Where troubles melt like lemon drops,
Away above the chimney tops,
That's where you'll find me . . .

Oh . . . the poor poor man.

Raymond Stop being fucking soft, he was an arse for using his Hoover in the garden. He was so damn precious about a few stray leaves, Jesus! He'd still be boring us . . . I'd happily see him under a bus.

India No need now.

Target One Jackie, Jackie, this is Target One, over.

Jackie Target One, you have Jackie, over.

Target One Jackie, switch channel 68, over.

Jackie 10-4, Jackie, switching to channel 68. Out.

Raymond holds the Pimms up. India lights a cigarette and stubs the old one out.

Raymond Anyone for another? Soft-arse?

Raymond fills India's glass up.

India Stop, stop /

Raymond Lets get buggered /

India Honestly, that's plenty.

Raymond Hen doesn't drink, whereas I have a penchant for a drink or two.

Raymond tops himself up. Thomas enters. They all look up.

India Our saviour is back!

Raymond Hello, hooligan.

Raymond pours Thomas a large drink and hands it to him.

India It's so much nicer with a bit of sun.

Thomas Apparently because we're in England, being Brits, we should expect shitty weather /

Raymond Some jobsworth, showing his knackers off, eh? Hope you stamped good 'nd proper, made the fucker squirm. I was in the bank, this spotty little prick served me . . . Kept farting on, spotty little fuck . . . Total bloody joke, world's gone crazy.

Here's to us, eh!

They raise their glasses.

Fuck the rest / of them.

Thomas Oh you arrived! Hello, Hen!

Thomas pats Henry's shoulder.

Henry Alright.

Raymond In a world run by arseholes, don't let them get you down!

India Ooh isn't this nice . . .

Henry puts the Kettle Chip down, stands up and gives India a hug.

What was that for? Hello, Henry!

Henry I've missed you so much, it's so nice to be back. I love you.

Henry sits with his arm round his mother.

Raymond Would you look at the wet blanket!

India No, it is. It is so nice, to sit here as a family . . . oh, my little Hen /

Raymond A toast, here's to Henry!

Everyone raises their glasses.

All To Henry!

Raymond May the little tosser live a successful and fruitful life . . .

They laugh and drink. India puts her cigarette out and lights another automatically.

Decent glass of Pimms. Not often, one can enjoy, decent glass of Pimms . . . the weather being as it has . . . not a lot of Pimms drinking being done, isn't the mince pie and mulled wine season upon us as I speak?

India We were at Tim thingy's house for dinner. They gave us mulled wine –

Raymond Fucking torture.

India His wife /

Raymond Has a fat arse, must mention the arse / on her.

India She cannot cook, gave out these enormous portions /

Raymond Huge blancmange of a woman /

India Far too much for one person /

Raymond Fuck the food, she ought to look in the mirror and have a damn good shave /

India Raymond's making her out as if she were Stalin. Little blonde thing above her lip, you'd struggle to notice.

Raymond Unlike her twitch, which used her face as a general play area. I told her, that's quite some twitch you're maintaining there, there were shrieks of laughter.

India Eye contact was rather difficult afterwards /

Raymond Highlight of the evening, never endured such boring conversation, I found myself winding him up.

India (*smirking*) Kept telling Tim his car was a rust bucket.

Raymond There's something wrong in his head – what's the medical equivalent of being a fucking arse? The man's blind, married himself off with a monster, you know proof in the pudding.

India The pudding wasn't that bad actually, profiteroles from M&S. I saw the packaging in the bin.

Raymond He's completely perverse. When we got down to the nitty gritty, clueless about cars. Cretin brought out some old Swedish go-cart, 'Top down, how's this for you, Ray?' I can't do it, I can't do his accent . . . kind of weird. 'Ray'no that's not it – 'Ray, Ray / Ray –'

India (*attempting the accent*) 'Ray / Ray, Raymond –'

Raymond Forget it you can't do it either. 'Ray, could you pass me the greens?' (*Laughs at his awful attempt.*)

India Hopeless /

Raymond The man couldn't drive his way out of a crisp packet. (*To Henry.*) Darling, eat with your mouth shut, you're making a fucking racket.

India stubs out her cigarette. She lights another cigarette. The stub smokes in the ashtray.

Add insult to injury, he got flashed by a speed trap while we were racing.

India exhales a thick fog of smoke.

India I find cars so boring.

A boat passes.

Thomas How many points did he lose?

Raymond I shouldn't think too many, the guy's a doctor /

India A vet, he's a vet.

Raymond He can say 'in a dash to pick the dingle berries from a sheep's arse'.

India smiles.

Henry Mum's smiling.

Thomas (*pointing at passing boat*) Hey, look Hen! It's all your Sloaney mates, give them a wave!

Raymond (*about passing boat*) These idiots are so tiresome. I hate these bloody gin palaces throwing their wake around.

Thomas What are they called?

Henry Who?

Thomas They all have dickhead names, go on, wave.

Henry I don't know them so why should I wave /

Thomas (*waving*) Oy, oy, slags!

What's that friend of yours, with a dick name?

India lights another cigarette.

Leopold.

Raymond Cock-wash, no one's called Leopold any more.

The VHF crackles into life. In the background of Lindsay Ann there's the sound of confusion and a girl's wailing. Messages broken up by white noise.

Lindsay Ann Mayday, mayday . . . this's vessel *Lindsay Ann*, calling Solent Coastguard.

The family register the request for help, but turn a blind eye to it.

India You know a Xan, darling –

Thomas (*imitating his father*) Cock-wash, no one's called Xan!

Henry Offer you a Reuben? Conrad broke his nose so we called him Reuben.

Lindsay Ann Mayday, *Lindsay Ann* calling Solent Coastguard . . .

Solent Coastguard Vessel calling the Coastguard . . . go ahead with your mayday . . . all other vessels stand by. Over.

Lindsay Ann Coastguard, this is Lindsay Ann . . . Our position 24,33 north . . . 74,56 west . . . Our boom's swung . . . caught . . . girl right . . . Smashed . . . glasses into her face . . . eyes . . . blood literally gone everywhere . . .

Thomas Fuck it, something fucking gay. Think knob.

Henry I'll try my best, knob, knob . . . no, no one called knob.

Solent Coastguard Go ahead *Lindsay Ann*. Over.

Lindsay Ann It just keeps like spurting . . . spurting . . . gash in her nose . . . 'cos every time y' know the boat . . . the bone starts er popping out, an' erm, panicking . . . girl's . . . throwing up, I'm erm . . . total loss, over.

Solent Coastguard 10-4, *Lindsay Ann*, remain calm . . . Don't try to stop the blood flow . . . risk doing permanent damage to her eyes. Go ahead with the type of vessel you're in. Over.

Thomas Fuck it, the only reason I'm thinking of Leopold is 'cos of Grampy's *Riva*.

Raymond Pappi's pride and joy. Lovely teak decking.

Thomas shakes his head.

Lindsay Ann Slipper 42 feet, green hull, white decks . . . four girls and me on board. Over.

India What do people feel like tomorrow?

Henry (*depressed*) Mum, let's not . . . tomorrow and tomorrow.

India exhales extravagantly.

I don't want to think about tomorrow.

Solent Coastguard 10-4, *Lindsay Ann*, we copy your distress call. Be advised help's on the way. This is Solent Coastguard, out.

Seagulls scream.

Thomas Come shooting with me?

Raymond Now now, you might want to retrieve that invitation. I was watching this young man, for what . . . the best part of half an hour last weekend, wouldn't you say Hen . . . you know what I'm getting at?

Henry Haven't got a clue.

India lights a cigarette.

Raymond I'm sure you do. Would you like to tell the lovely ladies and gentlemen what you got up to last weekend?

Henry Love to, if only I knew what you were bleating on about.

Raymond What I'm badgering on about is /

Henry No, oh yeah! No, I know what you're talking about, I was stalking a thistle. See there, it went down like a ton of bricks /

Raymond It was hysterical. Behind the fence, crawling in the long grass like a commando. Wearing this ridiculous bandana, rolling from side to side, oh and the disappointment when he found / out it was only a thistle

Henry Hey Dad the sun was in – (*Raising his voice.*) Oy, prick-head, listen Dad, the sun was in my eyes and it had things sticking up, shaped like ears, you know, how was I meant to know?

Raymond You should have seen him, what an arse!

Thomas Better luck tomorrow, just follow my lead.

Raymond 'The sun was in my eyes.'

India I'm sure it was.

Henry Actually it was, you just try looking into blazing sun, bet you'll find you have difficulty /

Raymond Had – and really Hen, I want to put emphasis on the *had* – if you *had* actually bagged something, you'd never killed it out right. The amount of time spent wringing necks, pulling heads / off /

Thomas No! That's not fair, he's not that bad. We went clay-pigeon shooting, didn't we? Hen was better than a lot of the girls.

Raymond Wonder how you'll fare in the army? Not too sure they won't end up sticking you in the kitchens, out of harm's way.

When I was in the armed services, way back now, but we used to play a bloody marvellous gag. One straight from the old Eton days. The classic prank had been to take the bloodied head from a dead rabbit. Put it inside the prefect's bed.

Sixth-formers used to be bloody tired from doing prefects' duty. Uh God, I remember being buggered by eleven o'clock you know – 'Matron, fuck the cocoa!' One would jump headlong into the sack without looking. We all used to wait for the scream – golly, and the screams we got.

Best were the ones who fell asleep, then woke up on their own at five a.m. with the, you know, old bloody head next to them. (*Laughs.*)

Lindsay Ann (*weak, desperate*) Kayliegh . . . Kayliegh . . .

    Thomas and Raymond poke Kettle Chips away.

Raymond Kettle Chips – bloody good, aren't they?

Lindsay Ann Come on girl, don't pass out . . .

Don't . . .

Stop touching . . . stop . . .

India Ray, turn it off.

    Raymond turns the radio off. India puts her cigarette out.

Henry How did it happen?

Raymond They must've been tacking, jived, boom swung. Smashed her specs into her face.

Thomas I rather want to know what happened to her.

Raymond Probably got her nose broken /

Thomas All squished to one side . . .

India Let's not talk about it, guys.

Beat.

Thomas How's the love-life, Hen? Who's the lucky slag?

Henry There's no lucky slag.

Thomas If you're interested . . . think you'd really get on with her.

Henry Pardon.

Thomas I met this chick at work, moderately hot. She's about your age, told her that my little brother was a desperate wanker /

Henry I'm not /

Thomas Slight interjection, we've all seen your collection of naughty forties.

Raymond You could make a valuable contribution to the British Library.

Thomas Please, I'll buy you *Mayfair*, anything. Let me, you're gonna go blind gawping at all that fudge.

Henry (*playing dumb*) I don't know . . . what're you talking about?

Thomas Hen, you don't even bother to hide them any more, they're scattered across the floor. I slipped 'nd nearly twisted my ankle on an issue of *Readers' Wives*. I shit you not, went in his porn den, a whore, full bondage gear, spiked heels and spank-paddle accosted me yesterday afternoon /

Henry I hope she beat the shit out of you.

India Actually Hen, on a more serious note, I was going to have a word because I'm sure Pat's embarrassed when she cleans your room /

34

Henry She doesn't clean my room.

India I stopped her going in, because of the mess /

Raymond Such an old prude, mess! It's only a bit of porn, jolly wholesome, good for the heart. Don't know why you insist on making such a fuss. Well, she's had a few nippers of her own. Just a natural part of growing up, when you think about it. Godsend when you think what he could be up to . . . Harmless bit of masturbation never hurt a fly. Hen's just a bit of a horn dog /

Henry Dad!

Raymond What /

India It's gratuitous.

Thomas (*laughing*) Hen's just a bit of a young horn dog /

Raymond It's affectionate, he likes it, you like it.

India lights another cigarette and stubs out a half-smoking one in the ashtray. Henry sighs.

Henry Fuck it. Prefer Hen.

Thomas Anyway, horn dog, I gave her your number and told her to give you a ring.

Henry You did what?

Raymond It would be nice to see you with a bit of crumpet on your arm.

You haven't had a girlfriend for a long time. What's the name of that young bird you used to hang about with?

Henry Sophie.

Raymond Sophie was quite something, had a soft spot for Sophie, didn't you? Well she was very fit, a real nut-cruncher, oh a lovely girl, very funny. You should ask her out on a dinner date /

Henry I don't do dinner dates, they're for wankers.

Raymond Way to a woman's heart is /

Henry Is through your wallet, yeah heard it all before, it's not true /

Raymond It is, honestly, I think you'll find, sad as it may seem, that the second you open your wallet, you'll see a certain young lady's legs parting.

India For goodness' sake.

Thomas (*mocking Raymond*) *So* young Hen, simplistic as it may seem, what we've learned today is the operative word for getting to a lady's pants /

Raymond Seriously, you mock me, Thomas, you mock me, but you could be queer . . . I often wonder, it has been a fair bit since you got any action.

Henry (*making a movement with his thumb*) Ha! Squish!

Raymond And as for you, Henry, pull your fucking finger out of your arse! I tell you, but you won't listen to me . . . Dear Lord, make me a day younger and I'd hit on her, the Sophie bird.

Henry You must've been made a day younger then.

Raymond Bring her round for tea some time /

Henry (*dogmatic*) No.

Raymond Mark my words, Hen, some day you'll kick yourself.

Thomas Hear hear! Here's to kicking yourself, Hen!

Lindsay Ann (*a girl*) No she can't, Kayliegh, can you hear us?

The family stop and listen.

Kayliegh?

Beat.

She's *my* friend alright . . . her eyelids are hanging off . . .

Raymond (*snorting*) Blind me.

India turns the radio off. Henry looks panicked.

India Thought I told you to turn that off.

Raymond I did, come on /

India I will not come on.

Henry (*panicked*) What's happened?

Raymond Oh, she can't see because she's got blood in her vision.

Henry Shouldn't we help . . . can't we help out /

Raymond Darlings, there's no point crying about it.

Henry Is she blinded?

Raymond Hardly, Hen! Bit of a bump, bruise, nothing special, more's the pity.

India Don't wind me up /

Raymond Bugger me! They are, stop fussing. If that moron tries to get at the glass, he'll only pull her retina out. Eye's a football, with jellyish stuff inside – yank at that, the whole lot 'll plop out . . . he can't do jack, she needs an eye surgeon.

Thomas Bet it probably looks pretty gory Hen, with her eyelids hanging off –

Henry Fuck off, cock-breath.

Thomas laughs.

Raymond None of this is unfixable, long as she doesn't fidget with her face.

Thomas That's all right then. Phew, Hen.

Raymond When what's-his-arse crashed his car, he got a face full of windscreen, had hamster cheeks and panda eyes for a couple of weeks, old fart's fine / now.

India Phil Mercer was virtually walking around with a white stick, for the best part of a year.

Raymond Please . . . that crash turned him into a nicer man, he was a cunt before.

India You can be impossible sometimes /

Raymond Crashing his car was the best thing he's ever done in my opinion.

Beat.

India The blood altered his vision /

Raymond Rather like trying to look through a glass of red wine.

Thomas A very good claret, a Margaux maybe /

India (*not taking part*) Said they looked like black dots and smudges. Philip was this close to being permanently blind.

Raymond (*irritated*) Cunt . . . I still haven't forgiven him for 'losing' my hedge-clippers. He lent the fuckers back to me, and I knew they were mine because /

India The yellow handles.

Thomas (*fat grin*) The ones with the fucking yellow handles oh . . . what a bastard!

Raymond It's the last time I lend anyone, repeat anyone, anything.

Beat.

Henry What about the girl . . . ?

Raymond (*conceited*) Listen to this . . . you can slice the eyeball in half, and it's no more painful than dropping a brick on your foot. The problem's panic, people panic in those situations. Get a load of girls screaming . . .

Thomas (*sarcastic*) Bloody girls, can't trust them /

Raymond Someone once faced a fast ball. I remember – uh there we were when crunch – I've missed a bit, some guy bowled . . . that's right, other guy belts it off leg side. That's right, bosh, straight in the eye, crunch, like a horse with an apple, of course he screamed like a baby. Blubbing out of the good eye . . . Girl who wears the green leotard, you know . . . took him to A&E, chain-smoked all the way there. Smoking – well there's a nasty plebby habit.

Beat. Raymond sighs and smiles.

Henry . . . Henry, Henry, what will we do with you?

Henry I don't know.

Raymond (*wry*) Stop smoking in the upstairs bathroom, I noticed you've started smoking up there again. I'll bloody hide the arse off you, got it?

Henry Got it.

Raymond stares at Henry.

Raymond You're very beautiful. One day, you'll be sixty, too. You'll look nothing like now . . . only something underneath your smile.

People who knew you once, they'll say . . . 'He hasn't aged.' 'He has preserved well.' 'Oh well very well.'

Raymond starts to see double. He places one hand over his left eye.

My brother goes through it all three years before me . . .
I look at him, to see which chunk of my hair will fall out
next. You'll look at Thomas, see how he crumbles before
he dies.

Thomas Thanks, Dad.

Raymond taps his hand on the table.

Raymond How it will be, huh? My children, nobody
knows . . . No one but me. Yes, I know – the world, sits
there for you, only for your beckoning. My boys, look,
by your elbows. See, it sits there, with such patience.

Henry Dad /

Raymond Nah, nah-ha, promise you. (*Thumbs on chest.*)
This old man is no longer young. I'm – just – saying –
you shall be . . .

*Raymond touches his scalp with his fingertips
momentarily, and then slowly raises them unto the
heavens.*

(*Slow.*) . . . great!

Henry quietly gets up, with no luck.

Where're you going?

Henry Nowhere.

Raymond (*hand over one eye*) Who are you! Oy, come
here, self-important little jerk, sit the fuck down!

India You're scaring him /

Raymond Y' tight-arsed little cunt! (*High and mighty.*)
Well, fuck off then, I don't want to know, fuck off, sod
off, fuck off.

Thomas Hen's embarrassed, Dad.

India lights another cigarette and stubs out the half-smoked one.

Raymond Nothing to wet his pants about. I'm telling the cunt how it will be.

Thomas Well the cunt doesn't want to hear, frankly. You're pissed.

Henry (*embarrassed*) No, it's just kind of late / I'm /

Raymond Go on – you go . . . go . . .

India stubs the barely smoked cigarette out and lights another.

Uh, fuck – off!

Henry and Raymond stare.

If you could see how beautiful you are.

Henry (*humble, quiet*) Thank you, can we go now?

Raymond No. This is an invitation please, come to my funeral, I want everyone – have a very good time, get jolly pissed – tables scattered here an' there . . . Invitations, on acid-free card, embossed lettering . . . You're coming to my funeral.

Silence. Raymond notes the silence.

I'm noting the silence.

And what a silence it is . . .

Beat.

Someone's missing . . .

India (*fake-cheerful*) Stop being a silly old goat. (*Haunted.*) Someone's missing.

Silence.

Raymond Kid, I got bad news. But I can't remember . . . any more.

I drank too much, didn't I?

Beat. Raymond lifts his head to Henry.

(*Caring.*) Ten o'clock this morning, everything went all so sad and pointless. I'm sorry.

India (*pained*) You're spoiling it.

Beat.

Thomas Dad, what is it?

Raymond stands swaying gently in the breeze, thinking.

You wanted to tell us something.

Beat.

Raymond (*holding himself back*) My dad took me out to the Needles, first boat trip, Pappi's dead now. Voice broke, think uh, I was twelve? Remember. (*Smiles.*) My memory. My voice broke at Godshill. There was a bathroom. It was green. It was a rented cottage. You're very important to me, Henry. You're going to have to look after me, I will look after you. When the sea gets rough, don't look at the water, churning all around you – no. It'll make you feel worse. Look at the horizon far away. It's the only stable thing.

Thomas How about I skipper?

Raymond What on earth would I want that for?

Thomas Just because, Jesus . . . you're just / drunk –

India Completely blind drunk, you can't take the helm like this.

Raymond Watch me, I can see fine, I'm fine.

Henry Dad, let Tom /

Raymond No, no, I'm good to go. I'm . . .

Raymond looks at the control desk. He doesn't recognise the buttons.

Yes . . . perfectly . . . fine. I'm all right.

Raymond sits, breathing heavily. His head slumps to one side.

Someone's making a bit of coffee? Give me a minute.

I'll go below, check the course.

Thomas stands.

Henry It's not out of our way to the Needles.

Raymond Never forget . . . those Needles, they are a monument to the dead . . . To all those brave men who drowned alone, out at sea. Pointlessly.

(*To India.*) Hold my hand.

India Thomas, start the engine.

Raymond India . . . I'm sorry.

India (*looking in the opposite direction, cold*) Have a Kettle Chip.

Thomas turns the engine on, it roars, he revs it. The lights snap to blackout, cold darkness. The quiet sound of seagulls. The sounds of the engine and seagulls diminish and are replaced by a voice in the distance, apologising – not clearly enough to hear word for word, just in the tone of the voice. A bird sings out, then is silent. A milk float comes to a halt, the milkman whistles aimlessly, the clink of milk bottles. The milk float fades into the distance. The sound of keys in a door, and then footsteps gradually approaching.

SCENE SIX

In the darkness a door opens, a figure enters, goes to the loo and urinates. After a moment.

India What are you doing, Henry?

Beat.

Henry Um . . . I think I'm taking a piss.

India Why are you pissing in the dark? You're probably pissing on the seat.

Henry The lights fused when I switched them on earlier.

India Wouldn't you like the lights on?

Henry Yes.

Beat. The lights come up: a bathroom. India lies in the bath, the water up to her neck. She has a wet green face-pack on. The bath is completely full of white bubbles.

India Hello, Henry.

Henry Hello.

India Was your nightmare scary, darling?

Henry (*slow*) Yeah . . . How do you know about my nightmare?

India Do you want to tell me about it?

Henry Yeah, we were . . . on the boat. It was a weekend, I'd come back from school.

Think we were drinking Pimms? No, you were drinking Pimms and I was drinking Diet Coke for some reason . . . Mum?

India Yes?

Henry And I was over the moon, 'cos I could see you all, in front of me. We all talked and joked . . . There is a girl on another boat, a girl had been hurt. Everything is going kind of nasty and I want to wake up. I can hear she is hurt badly, and I want to help her, Dad gets pissed somehow . . . Then you see, he wants to tell us something. He can't remember what it is . . . And I know what he's trying to tell us, he wanted . . . Tell me you're dead but he's too drunk . . . He can't think straight. You're dead, aren't you?

Henry smiles, slowly walks to her. He puts his hand out to her.

Can I touch you?

India Of course you can, this is your dream, isn't it?

Henry touches India.

Henry I'm touching you. Oh . . . Mum, it's so fucking good to see you, it's so fucking great.

India It's nice to see you too, Hen.

Henry I have so many fond memories of you.

Didn't ever dare tell myself how much I'd miss you. I remember the look before you kiss me. The sound of keys in the front door meant you were home and everything was safe . . .

I'm a small child, standing in a corridor. There are voices, they are happy. They say my name and I can see the front door at the end of the passage. I can see Thomas. I'm too excited, my head won't keep still. We're going somewhere.

India Going for a walk –

Henry I don't know, but I look down . . . and there you are, putting my shoes on, doing up the laces. Your face is smiling at me.

India smiles.

India Now don't let me forget, Henry, I've come for a reason. I've got to give you something for the rest of your life that will give you good luck. Hey and another thing Hen.

Henry Yup.

India Darling, please stop taking God so seriously.

Henry I don't /

India He really wouldn't want it, He's not like that.

Henry No.

India You're going to have to take Him a lot less seriously. Let's make that a number-one rule.

Henry OK . . . Oh Mum . . .

India It's so good to see you, Hen . . . Come on, sweetie, everything will be alright. Give me a hug.

Beat.

Henry But you're dead.

India That doesn't matter, come on, hug me.

Henry Why do people have to die?

India Henry, we all have to die, at some point.

Henry But why?

India Darling, if we didn't, life wouldn't be worth living, um . . . but it took a long time for me to see that. I was a lot older than you . . .

Beat.

46

What are you thinking about? This is the nice bit, you don't have to be scared.

Henry Because . . . because I'm so scared of dying, and death . . .

India That's so silly, you're not going to die for a long time, honey bun /

Henry And people are horrible and stupid . . . There's a kind of blindness.

India Darling, you're just not looking at it properly. If only you would see that . . .

Dear God! Sometimes people can be very generous and kind.

All you have to do is ask, and I'll be right at your side because I love you. You will feel me there, um, even in the blackest nightmare.

Henry Is it . . . It's all going to be alright, isn't it?

India When you die, you'll be an old man, you'll want to die. Your family will be all around you, your wife and your children um, and who knows even your children's children.

Henry My family will be around me.

India Yes . . .

Beat.

Good luck, darling.

Goodbye.

Henry Why?

India Because it's time for you to wake up. You've got school to go to.

Henry But I don't want to, I don't want you to go.

India Henry . . . please don't be difficult. I've got to go.

Henry I love you so much, Mum.

India Give me a smile, Hen.

Henry smiles. Beat.

Be brave, you're going to do fine . . .

(*Slow.*) How old I feel.

India rubs the now-dry face mask. Dust falls from her face.

Henry It took one week for you to die, one Sunday to another.

India's head tilts to one side. One hand grips the side of the bath, the other reaches out; it roams of its own accord. She speaks, but her voice has totally changed: it is very dull, the words are sleepy.

India Get me that down darling . . . heavenly seven and a half . . . yes . . . But look at the sheer quantity of them . . . the poor people . . . Closed again, open the window . . .

Henry They asked if I wanted to watch any more . . . but I couldn't . . . I bent down and kissed your forehead. As I walked away, through the swing doors, I rubbed your kiss from my lips.

What am I meant to think?

My mum died, it took one week in the end . . .

Slowly India slides under the water.

My mother made me nasturtium sandwiches, I keep coming back to that.

India is completely under the water. Henry stares at the empty bath. The dim sound of seagulls, the roaring

*of an engine, growing as the lights fade to black.
Through the roaring of engines we hear:*

Lindsay Ann Solent Coastguard, this is vessel *Lindsay
Ann*, ETA? Over.

Solent Coastguard *Lindsay Ann*, ETA of one minute.
How's the victim's vision? Over.

Sound of engine fades, VHF becomes clearer.

Lindsay Ann Coastguard . . .

Solent Coastguard *Lindsay Ann*?

Lindsay Ann (*Kayliegh's shaky voice replaces the
skipper*) I've got blood in my hair, boat keeps jolting 'nd
every . . . everything's really blurred, outlines moving
about, shorelines 'nd masts . . . lights flashing off the
water . . . 'S like they turned the light on in the middle
of the night . . . Someone shadowy keeps coming in . . .
My feet are so frozen . . .

Solent Coastguard *Lindsay Ann*, help's on the way.

*The sound of the radio disappears, the sound of
seagulls rises. The click of a light switch and all the
lights, house lights included, come on full – intense
brightness. Blinding lights aimed at the audience. A
bleached moment, then the lights fade till they show . . .*

*A dim lamp with a red lampshade, Henry sitting in a
recliner chair. Peter staring at him. The lights continue
to fade.*

Blackout.